DEATH OF THE
Dinosaurs

Written by Herbie Brennan

Illustrated by Chris Brown and Roger Simó

Contents

Introduction

Dinosaurs first appeared on Earth more than 250 million years ago. For most of that time these enormous animals roamed throughout the world.

They were the kings of this planet. Humans, who appeared much later, are just four million years old at the most.

Dinosaurs had no natural enemies. Yet, 65 million years ago, they disappeared.

The big question is **Why?**

There are two main theories about what happened to the dinosaurs. Scientists have been arguing about theories for years.

Theory One:
The Great Disaster Theory

Theory Two:
The Slow Death Theory

The Great Disaster Theory

This is what some scientists believe:

A giant lump of rock, or **meteor**, from outer space crashed into Earth about 65 million years ago.

The crash was so violent that it left a huge dent (called a **crater**) on the surface of Earth.

When something like that happens, huge amounts of dirt and dust are thrown high up into the air.

There was so much dust that it blocked out the light and heat of the Sun for many months, perhaps even years.

Without sunlight, plants could no longer grow.

Some dinosaurs ate plants. They needed tons of plants each day, so they died first when the plants disappeared.

As the plant-eating dinosaurs died, the meat-eaters who hunted them had less and less to eat.

The dust cleared at last and the Sun shone again, but by then it was too late for the dinosaurs. They had all starved to death.

It might have happened even faster than that. Some scientists believe dinosaurs needed sunshine to warm them up. If this was so, they would have died from the cold even before the food ran out.

Fossil skeletons tell us about the dinosaurs that died.

Evidence For The Great Disaster Theory

What evidence do scientists have for this theory?

When scientists dug down to what was the surface of Earth 65 million years ago, they found a layer of metal called **iridium**.

Iridium is very rare on Earth's surface. It is much more common in rocks in outer space.

Iridium can be seen in this layer of rock.

Scientists also found a type of brittle rock, called **quartz**, at the same level as the iridium. The quartz had cracks in it. The cracks were the sort you would expect to find if something struck Earth very hard.

Scientists also discovered lots of glass beads that they thought had been formed in the explosion when the meteor struck Earth.

A close-up photo of cracked quartz

USA

MEXICO

Then, in
June 1990,
scientists found an
enormous crater in Mexico.
They believe the crater was
made by a meteor that
crashed to Earth 65 million
years ago.

SOUTH
AMERICA

Theory Two:

The Slow Death Theory

However, some scientists believe another theory.

This is what they believe:

At the time the dinosaurs appeared on Earth, there was only one enormous stretch of land on the whole planet. The dinosaurs roamed across almost every part of it.

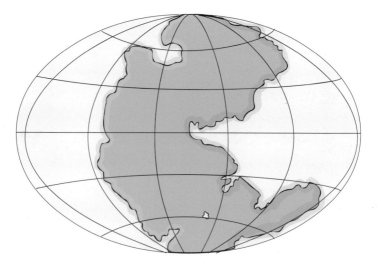

This enormous land mass, called Pangaea, existed over 200 million years ago.

Over millions of years, though,
this great mass of land started
to break up very slowly.

During the break-up, volcanoes
erupted and sea levels rose and fell.

The weather changed.
The world had been hot,
but now it turned cold.

All this brought changes in the type of plants that could grow and the sort of animals that could live on Earth.

The dinosaurs could not cope with their new surroundings.

The number of dinosaurs slowly got smaller. At last, they died out altogether.

Theory Two:

Evidence For The Slow Death Theory

What evidence do scientists have for this theory?

This crack in Earth's surface shows where two continents are moving apart.

Scientists now know that all the **continents** of the world are moving apart very, very slowly.

Pangaea

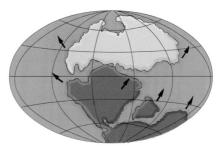

About 100 million years ago

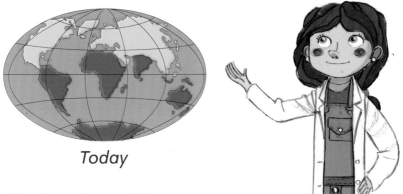

Today

The break-up of Pangaea

Scientists can tell that there was once a time
when all the continents were pressed together
in one great mass of land. If you look at a
world map today, you can see how well Africa
once fitted up against North America and
South America, like pieces of a jigsaw puzzle.

fossils found on high land

sea

Fossils of sea creatures have been found on high land and low land. This shows that the sea levels rose and fell millions of years ago.

Fossil of a fish

Scientists have studied layers of melted rock, called **lava**, which is produced when volcanoes erupt. The lava shows that many volcanoes must have erupted at the time that the dinosaurs disappeared.

Lava flowing from a volcano

Which Theory Is Right?

A problem for scientists is that the same evidence can be used to support both the Great Disaster Theory and the Slow Death Theory.

A meteor crashing into Earth will produce glass beads, iridium, and cracks in quartz.

Volcanoes erupting will also produce glass beads, bring up iridium from deep inside Earth, and cause cracks in quartz.

In the years ahead, scientists might find evidence for a new theory. Perhaps they will find evidence that will settle the matter once and for all. Until they do though, the argument continues.

Glossary

continents   main masses of land on Earth's surface

crater   bowl-shaped hole made by a meteor crashing into Earth

iridium   metal found deep inside Earth and in objects from space, but rarely on Earth's surface

lava   melted rock flowing from a volcano

meteor   rock from space

quartz   type of crystal rock

Index

Published by Pearson Education Limited, 80 Strand, London, WC2R 0RL.

www.pearsonschools.co.uk

Text © Herbie Brennan 2001

Designed by Andrew Magee Design Ltd
Character art by Roger Simó 2016
Illustrated by Chris Brown and Roger Simó

First published 2001

20 19 18 17 16
10 9 8 7 6 5 4 3 2 1

British Library Cataloguing in Publication Data
A catalogue record for this book is available from the British Library

ISBN 978 0 435 18059 1

Printed and bound in the UK by Ashford Colour Press

Acknowledgements

The publisher would like to thank the following for their kind permission to
reproduce their photographs:

(Key: b-bottom; c-centre; l-left; r-right; t-top)
Alamy Images: artpartner-images.com 8, Douglas Peebles 19br, Gary
Moseley 10t, Michelle Gilders 9, Tom Bean 16; **Science Photo Library Ltd:**
David A Hardy 11b, 20, Dirk Wiersma 10b; Shutterstock.com: beboy 13, 21, 22,
MaxFx 11t, miha de 12, 17t, psamtik 18b

All other images © Pearson